Rearing Backyard Meat Rabbits:

Complete Step By Step Practical Guide Raising Rabbits

Alfred Walker

Table of Contents

Introduction

The notion of raising rabbits for profit is not new. Since ancient times, people have been rearing rabbits as pets and sustenance. This company is incredibly simple to start; even novices can do it.

We must develop new methods of food production to meet the needs of an expanding population. The "Micro-Livestock" rabbit may be a fantastic source of food production. Commercial production of rabbits is a tremendous possibility for farming and maybe a major source of revenue and employment.

Rabbits need a little dwelling space and little food to survive. Compared to other varieties of animal meat, rabbit meat has a higher ratio of protein, calories, calcium, and vitamins. Additionally, it has less salt, fat, and cholesterol than other meat.

Their meat is incredibly flavorful, filling, and simple to digest for individuals of all ages. Rabbit meat consumption is also not prohibited by any religion. Rabbits have a rapid rate of growth, and each time a mother produces 2 to 8 young. They have the capacity to transform low-quality food into high-quality meat, skin, or fiber.

For farmers without access to land and educated jobless individuals, raising rabbits may be an excellent source of income. Therefore, the commercial rabbit farming industry may be a fantastic way to fulfill the need for food or protein and a terrific way to create jobs. In this book, we outline the benefits of commercial rabbit farming as well as the procedures for getting started.

Chapter 1

Rabbit Caging System

The conventional method of raising rabbits was in a hutch that was put in the garage, basement, or backyard. The house rabbit setup is, however, addressed here more in-depth since, in recent years, the population of house rabbits has far overtaken that of hutch rabbits.

Because illnesses of neglect are widespread in rabbits abandoned in hutches at the rear of the yard, the enclosure should be easily accessible if rabbits are kept outdoors, either in a hutch for permanent housing or a pen for temporary habitation.

Pens should have a non-slip surface, and for increased absorbency, they may be furnished with straw, shredded paper, or hay. Sawdust or shavings are not recommended since they produce dust, which may irritate the respiratory system.

It is advised to clean portable components outside the rabbitry building. Protect the bunnies from the most potent cleaning solutions. More efficient cleaning techniques for equipment include using strong disinfectants, thorough soaking, and extended sun exposure.

Galvanized iron is a durable material that is simple to clean and disinfect.

Cages (hutches) with straw litter

Breeding animal cages should have a minimum of a 60 to 70 cm 80 to 100 cm 50 to 60 cm high floor area. Similar cages are often used to nourish five to six baby rabbits (to 2.5 to 2.8 kg). Cages that are a little bit higher should be utilized for the "deep litter" method. An equal layer of straw should be placed on top of bedding made of an absorbent substance (minimum thickness: 15 to 20 cm) such as husk or wood shavings. The whole system, including the absorbent layer and collected trash, has to be changed every six to seven weeks.

Cages (hutches) without litter.
Less-cluttered floors (hard earth or wooden planking). Despite regular cleaning, hygienic circumstances are almost always possible (uncontrolled local humidity favors parasitism). Because of the health dangers, this method is not advised. Therefore, it is

advised to lift the rabbits above the ground on a wire-mesh or slatted floor.

The wire-mesh floors should be thick enough not to injure the pads of the rabbits' feet (diameter 2.4 mm, minimum 2 mm); the mesh should be wide enough to let the droppings fall through (diameter 1 to 1.3 cm, according to feed) but narrow enough to prevent the feet getting caught in the mesh.

CAGE SYSTEMS

The accessibility, surveillance, and comfort that cage systems provide the animals are wonderful, and they also make waste management simple. The construction of cages without litter, which are mostly cages with wire-mesh flooring, is often made of metal or wood (the latter of which is out of the rabbits' reach). Although it is not required, wire mesh is often used across the whole wall.

There are four main systems:

- flat-deck,
- Californian,
- inclined-slope battery, and
- compact battery.

Flat-deck type of cages

The cages in this arrangement are all on the same level. Typically, they open from the top. They may be supported by low walls, feet, or chains. Floor debris falls into pits (ranging in depth from 20 cm to 1.5 m). Deep trenches are cleansed once every one to three years, but shallow pits are every two to three days.

The advantages of the flat-deck system are:

- Convenient animal handling and monitoring.
- Long lifespan of the utilized materials.
- The comfort of the producer's animals.
- There is no need for a complex ventilation system.

Californian type of cage

The cages in this design are staggered, with one deck elevated but not over the other. The upper level's cages open in the front, while the lower level's cages open at the top (poorer access). As in the flat-deck design, floor litter falls under the cages and is collected.

California's system has the following benefits:

similar airflow benefits to those of a flat deck.

Animal density per square meter of the building has slightly increased.

Drawbacks:

- Difficult surveillance and access to higher cages;
- More costly than a flat-deck frame.

Inclined-slope battery type of cages

Cages are stacked one on top of the other.

Waste is physically scraped from troughs using scrapers or flowing water after sliding down Ferro cement or metal panels into them.

The front of the cages opens.

The following benefits of the inclined slope:

- Increased animal density.
- Affordable price, while being more costly than flat-deck.

Drawbacks:

- Now matter the panels' construction type or how sharply they tilt,
- Improper garbage drops need frequent raking down;
- A high animal density needs appropriate ventilation;
- It is more difficult to supervise, handle, and get access to the cages.

Compact battery type of cage

Conveyor belts or vats placed underneath the cages and emptied by cable-operated scrapers may be used to collect animal feces (manual or electric). The cages must open from the front, much like the inclined-slope battery.

The advantage of this system is that the maximum density of animals reduces costs per animal housed.

Drawbacks:

- Regarding ventilation, cage access, animal surveillance, and animal handling in an inclined-slope battery;
- Quicker material degradation;
- Automatic scraping carries a risk of malfunction and dangerous scraper gas emissions;
- Inadequate lighting for breeding does.

Chapter 2

Breeds and Breeding

Selecting the ideal rabbit breed may be difficult since there are so many different types, sizes, colors, and personalities of rabbits. There are 50 distinct kinds of rabbits recognized by the American Rabbit Breeders Association (ARBA), from the jovial Californian rabbit to the beautiful English Lop.

They are essentially divided into groups based on their geographic origins and gene characteristics.

Choosing a Breed Based on Your Objective

What you want to do with your rabbits will determine the breeds you maintain and breed. The top breeds for each of the following purposes are listed below:

- Meat: Californian, New Zealand, Silver Foxes
- Fiber: Angora
- Pet: Flemish Giants, Rexes, Polish, Dutch

Each of these varieties will procreate successfully, but most rabbitries prefer the meat breeds since they produce big litters. They generate the greatest number of kits and the greatest amount of meat per adult rabbit.

When to Breed Rabbits

Due to potential issues, it is advised to wait until rabbits are at least 6 months old before breeding them.

In contrast to many other animals, rabbits may breed all year round. Their menstrual cycle is distinctive! If they haven't been bred, they won't ovulate. In actuality, breeding causes ovulation to occur.

Having said that, there are periods when does are more amenable to breeding.

How to Choose Your Breeding Pairs

It's crucial to choose pairings of objects that have the same size. A challenging pregnancy might arise from breeding a big buck with a petite doe. The doe may be unable to bear huge kits.

It's wise to avoid interbreeding between big and small breeds by mating rabbits of the same breed with one another.

Additionally, never cross-breed kits made from the same kindling. A doe, however, as well as bucks and does, may be bred back to the buck that gave birth to them. It's known as in-line breeding.

Most in-line breeding aims to emphasize the positive characteristics of the two rabbits who were selected to breed. But always remember that inbreeding may sometimes accentuate unfavorable qualities, so make your choice wisely.

How to Get The Buck's Hutch Breeding Ready

It is ideal to breed your rabbits on firm ground when the time comes. In hyperactive rabbits, wire-bottomed cages may grab toenails or even feet, resulting in significant harm.

If you only have cages with wire bottoms, put a temporary hardwood floor in the buck's cage for breeding, then take it out. Additionally, remove any feeders or waterers to offer the rabbits more space and prevent them from being entangled in them.

Finally, since does are very possessive of their territory and may behave violently against your buck, always take the doe to the buck's cage.

The Processes Involved in Rabbit Breeding

It's time to start the actual breeding procedure now that you know how to choose and prepare your bunnies for it!

1. Rabbits Sexing

Although it is a difficult process, sexing rabbits may be mastered with sufficient practice. It's difficult to tell males from females, and to make things worse, holding your bunnies while sexing them is much more difficult. This just makes the procedure more tiresome.

Compared to older rabbits, young bunnies are more challenging to mate. Although you may try to have sex with them when they're young, it's ideal to wait until they are fully grown. at least until you are confident in your abilities.

This is how you do it:

- With your other hand or arm, gently raise your rabbit while holding it by the scruff of the neck.
- Lay the rabbit on its back with its back supported (cradle your rabbit in your arms).
- If you hold your bunny firmly, it will unwind.
- Apply pressure to the vent with your middle and forefingers to make the genitals slightly protrude.
- The protuberance is visible: Bucks have a tube, while does have a small, pink-lined slit.

2. Pairing Up Your Rabbits

The breeding procedure will start after the doe is in the buck's cage. The buck may stamp his feet while the two rabbits chase and smell each other. You'll hear grunting, squeaking, and other endearing bunny noises you didn't know existed.

For support and to maintain the doe in position, the buck will mount her and bite the back of her neck. He's not harming her, so don't be alarmed.

The doe will lie on her stomach and show the buck her backside if she is open to being approached. In contrast, if she doesn't want to be bred, she may sit up and keep her bottom hidden from the male.

Carefully remove the doe as quickly as possible if the buck or doe exhibits hostile behavior against one another. Never lock rabbits in a cage together against their will or leave them unsupervised. If you do, you could be responsible for death.

If your buck falls off of your doe after mating with her, you can tell.

Indeed, it is rather spectacular. He frequently grunts or squeals before rolling to one side of her. Don't worry, he's OK.

We often allow our buck to mate with our does at least three times during a breeding session just to be safe. He normally feels fairly exhausted after the second time, however. Fast results may be obtained with good money.

Take the doe out of the cage and put her back on her own once they have successfully bred. Replacing the feed and water dishes will therefore save you money. He'll have a thirst.

3. Is The Doe Carrying Baby?

Although there are telltale signals that your doe is expecting, none of them are certain without an ultrasound.

Some signs that your doe could be pregnant are listed below:

When you gently press on her belly, you can feel the babies.

She has become heavier (weigh her before she is bred and 2 weeks after)

A week before kindling, she begins to build her nest.

Take your doe to your veterinarian for a reliable response if you want to be certain and safe.

4. The box of Doe's nesting supplies

When does begin to construct their nests, they jump about in an endearing manner. However, if does lack the necessary "equipment," they might be unable to properly care for their kits. You are responsible for making sure they have a warm, draft-free nesting box accessible for at least a week before their lighting.

The scent of other animals or rabbits shouldn't emanate from the nesting box. A nesting box should be well cleaned if it has been used for anything else before being offered to your doe. Give the doe enough time to get used to the nesting box in her cage.

The doe should be given straw or this soft nesting material so she may build her own nest. Don't worry about creating the nest for her; she will make it on her own.

The doe will begin collecting the nicest straw for her nest a few days before giving birth. She will then start working on creating a safe sanctuary for her young.

5. Pregnancy and Kindling

Giving or taking a few days, it takes around 30 days from the time a doe is bred to kindling. The doe should not be handled often throughout the pregnancy, and her nesting box should not be disturbed.

You should give your doe a bit extra food than normal, but not too much. Pregnant women who overfeed risk miscarriages and often deliver one or two obese offspring. Therefore, gradually increase her food intake while giving her plenty of water and roughage.

Your doe will start removing fur from her body a week or so before giving birth in order to insulate her nest. Given that some women start pulling two weeks before they kindle, this is an excellent technique to determine if she is pregnant.

As a result, if your doe isn't building a nest, try not to get discouraged. Some people do leave for work just before lighting.

Pulling fur may sometimes be a false alarm, as a side note. Some creatures create lovely nests while carrying out fraudulent pregnancies. These deceptive actions might be the result of a miscarriage or the mimicking of adjacent pregnant does.

The Doe's Pregnancy and Aftercare: How to Take Care of It.

You won't probably be there when your doe gives birth. It's amazing how often things start at night or when nobody is there to pry. As this is a crucial period for your doe, it is better to leave her alone in any case. She may miscarry or consume her infants if she grows anxious.

I know it's a dreadful thing to think about and much harder to see, but keep in mind that your bunny is an animal and sometimes has no idea what or why she is doing anything.

Make every effort to let nature run its course.

Check the doe's water supply once the kits are delivered and keep an eye on her from a distance. If all goes well, she will tidy up and start feeding her kits by herself.

If she isn't always in the nesting box with her young, don't be concerned. After giving birth, she would give herself breaks and require time to recover.

Allow the doe to take care of her kits on her own in the spirit of letting nature take its course as mom will do all the labor-intensive work. When necessary, she will give them food, wrap them in warm fur, and wean them as soon as it is appropriate.

You simply need to be concerned with keeping the cage tidy and the feeders stocked.

Babies are born without fur, but by looking at the color of their skin, you can usually tell what colors they will be.

Within 10 days of birth, kits begin to open their eyes. After around two weeks, it's common to observe them jumping out of their nest.

Chapter 3

Handling Unfortunate Complications

There will be times when kindlings fail, as with all things. When your doe doesn't behave or produce a litter as predicted, it is difficult to observe or manage.

If does who have never given birth before are unsuccessful as mothers the first time around, they should be granted a pass. They could have been immature or just unprepared. Young does sometimes neglect their young or, worse, devour them, for reasons that we do not fully understand.

Check out this list of typical issues and how to deal with each one:

1. *Eating Infants*

If you want to breed rabbits for a long time, you will see at least one of your does swallow her young, therefore I want you to be ready for the horrifying sight. Cannibalism may occur for a variety of causes, but it usually results from inexperience or a lack of maternal traits.

However, even if the doe has eaten her young, she will be OK. But if there are still live kits, think about delivering them to a doe that is nursing.

Weighing your alternatives is important since using a foster doe might be dangerous. For instance, the doe could murder the young, even her own. Not all does' nests will be amenable to foreign odors or sickly kits.

2. Children Born Outside the Nesting Box

When kits are scattered about the cage rather than their cozy nest, first-time moms are often to blame. The doe may have just been unsure about where to place them or what to do with them.

Does with lovely nests had given birth on the chilly floor of the cage. Who knows what screw on that one came loose, then!

You may pick up the infants and put them back in the nesting box if they are still alive. Try to warm them up in your hands or with a heat source if they are chilly.

The newborns may sometimes barely be breathing from the cold, but warmth immediately gives them life again. Return them to the nest as soon as they are warm. If you're fortunate, mom will likely handle the situation from there.

3. Too Many Infants

An excessively large litter might sometimes be too much for a doe to bear. The runts often land at the bottom of the pile and are unable to reach their mother's teet. Typically, they die of starvation.

4. Infections and Miscarriage

There is always a chance for difficulties before, during, and after giving birth, just as with the majority of mammals. Monitor symptoms of probable sickness by keeping an eye out for tiredness, lack of appetite, and water intake.

If you feel that your doe is unwell, consider bringing her to the doctor for assessment,

and make sure to keep her separate from
healthy bunnies.

Numerous factors, such as poor diet,
inclement weather, sickness, stress, and
others, may cause miscarriages. As soon as
you can, remove the fetuses from the doe's
cage to stop the spread of germs and illness.

Chapter 4

Nutrition

Rabbits are tiny herbivores with unique digestion and nutritional demands. They are picky feeders and prefer young plant shoots and nutrient-rich leaves over older plant material that is richer in fiber. Therefore, rabbits are regarded as concentrate pickers because they innately choose meals that are greater in energy density, which makes them more likely to become obese in captivity. In terms of anatomy, rabbits have an expanded hindgut and are non-ruminant herbivores (hindgut fermenters). A colony of bacteria that utilizes nutrients not digested in the small intestine is supported in the big cecum.

The gram-positive Bacteroides sp. makes up the majority of the bacteria in the cecum. Due to this, the rabbit is very susceptible to oral antibiotics; their treatment may disrupt the Bacteroides population and result in severe GI disturbances. In the hindgut, digests are divided according to particle size. Large particles (>0.5 mm), predominantly lignocellulose, are swiftly transported by peristaltic activity through the colon and eliminated as hard fecal pellets. This is the diet's "indigestible fiber" portion.

The maintenance of the cecum and colon's motility is the clinical significance of a diet rich in long particle length. Because they mechanically increase GI motility, this is why these fibers are sometimes referred to as the "scratch factor." Smaller particles (0.3 mm) and liquid substances are moved into the cecum by antiperistaltic activity, where they are fermented. This dietary element is referred to as "digestible" or "fermentable" fiber. The cecal contents are periodically released as "soft feces" or cecotrophs, which the rabbit consumes straight from the anus. When rabbits are given a diet rich in indigestible fiber, cecotroph intake is at its maximum. This material is swallowed again and supplies microbial protein, vitamins (including all the necessary B vitamins), and trace amounts of volatile fatty acids, which are crucial for the nutrition of rabbits. However, because the protein demands of the rabbits are only partially met by the amino acids gained in this way (especially for young, developing rabbits), the diet must provide the other amino acids, even though the necessary amino acid requirements for rabbits have not yet been established.

Vitamins A, D, and E must be consumed daily. B vitamins and vitamin K are adequately produced by gut bacteria; thus, dietary supplements are not required. The daily vitamin needs may rise due to illness and stress. Vitamins A and E are more easily destroyed by oxidation than other vitamins, thus it is important to prepare and store feed in a way that will minimize oxidation losses. Alfalfa meal makes up around 30% of most diets, which usually suffices for vitamin A. Vitamin A levels in the diet must range between 5,000 and 75,000 IU/kg. Excessive levels may result in resorbed litters, fetal hydrocephalus, and abortion. Lack of vitamin E has been linked to prenatal and neonatal mortality, muscular dystrophy, and infertility. It's possible that pet rabbit diets supplied in pet shops or even in bulk at feed stores don't rotate enough, which might lead to nutritional deficiencies. It's possible that the hay that was intended for tiny creatures had been on the shelf for a while.

Water Consumption Needs

In metabolic experiments, it has been shown that a rabbit would drink water at a rate of around 120 mL/kg/day. This is about double what is typically computed for a dog or cat of the same size. When you take into account the physiology of the GI tract and metabolic scaling, the increased water consumption makes sense. For at least 24 hours while they are in the hospital, dehydrated rabbits should get twice the maintenance fluids (240 mL/kg/day, or 10 mL/kg/hr). The majority of the time when a rabbit is diagnosed with anorexia, it is also dehydrated. A rabbit will consume substantially more water from an open bowl than from a sipper bottle, according to research.

Calculating Calorie Intake

The animal's basal metabolic rate (BMR) must first be determined in order to determine the daily maintenance calorie requirement for a rabbit. BMR is calculated as follows: BMR is equal to kW to the power of 0.75 (BMR = kcal/kg/day; k = constant in kcal/kg; W = weight in kg; the constant in k is 70 for placental animals). The BMR is the number of calories required only to keep the rabbit alive, without taking the clinical presentation into account. The sickness factor, which ranges from 1.2 to 2.0, is multiplied by the BMR to account for metabolic requirements above maintenance. Growth raises metabolic rate as well (illness factor of 1.5–3.0). However, famine and emaciation slow down the metabolism, reducing the need for calories (illness factor of 0.5–0.9).

Rabbit Carbohydrates

In rabbit diets, the function of carbs is often oversimplified, and generalizations like "carbohydrates are harmful to rabbits" don't provide a whole picture. It is debatable if adult rabbits are sensitive to high-starch diets, and it is uncertain whether starch acts as a risk factor for dysbiosis. Adult rabbits, on the other hand, seem to digest starch more effectively than young ones, according to research. Young rabbits have been observed to develop diarrhea when exposed to polysaccharides, such as gluco-oligosaccharides (starches that release glucose after breakdown). Other starches, such as galacto-oligosaccharides (short chains of galactose, found in the prebiotics group) and fructo-oligosaccharides (composed of short chains of fructose, found in many fruits and vegetables, such as onion, chicory, garlic, asparagus, banana, and many others), do not have the same effect.

Fructo-oligosaccharide-supplemented diets were shown to reduce morbidity in rabbits following the introduction of pathogenic Escherichia coli. Fructo-oligosaccharides are now included in many meals for rabbits as a result. Additionally, research has shown that developing rabbits can handle 15% of the molasses in the chow. Additionally high in calcium, iron, and magnesium is molasses.

Pelletized Feed

To create pellets, the components must be combined and then ground into a cylinder. Extruded or expanded diets are cooked to create a paste, which is then forced into a shaped pellet. The coarse grinding preserves the longer fibers in the food. Food that has been extruded produces a light biscuit. The benefit is that long-fiber particles may be added without the pellets crumbling and becoming friable. The raw materials are heated during cooking to improve the digestion of the starch. Extruded diets are also more flavorful and easily digested than pelleted rations. In order to avoid obesity or hypercalciuria, pelleted diets should be provided in accordance with the manufacturer's instructions.

Fibre Levels Recommended for Rabbits

Digestible fiber is crucial for GI motility stimulation, behavioral issues prevention (such as fur chewing), dental wear, hunger stimulation, and the consumption of cecotrophs. For pet rabbits, up to 20% of crude fiber with 12.5% indigestible fiber is often advised. Crude fiber is not useful for figuring out fermentable or digestible fiber since it primarily measures the lignin and cellulose component of the diet (indigestible fiber).Sanitation

Cleaning frequency depends on the type of facility or caging system. Rabbits typically choose a preferred latrine site, such as a corner of the cage. This normal behavior can be exploited during litter box training. A strategically placed litter box is readily accepted by most pet rabbits. Sanitation is especially important in rabbit production. Poor sanitation leads to disease and death; therefore, cleaning and sanitizing must be constant. Nest boxes must be disinfected between uses. Cages, feeders, and watering equipment should be sanitized periodically with an effective and inexpensive sanitizing solution such as diluted household chlorine bleach (1 oz/1 quart water) or other less corrosive disinfectants. Complete cleaning should be performed before housing new stock.

Frequent manure removal is essential. Excess manure leads to unacceptable levels of ammonia in the air, which predisposes to respiratory disease if housed indoors. In an outside setting, the buildup of fecal matter can attract a large number of flies, which can be the cause of the fly strike. The manure can be composted in an efficient pit system.

Chapter 5

Common Rabbit Diseases, Prevention and Treatment

By being aware of what a healthy rabbit needs and the subtle signals that might alert you to your rabbit's illness, you can avoid some of the frequent illnesses and disorders encountered in rabbits. Rabbits make fantastic domestic pets, but it's important to keep in mind that they are closely related to wild rabbits and, as a result, won't show symptoms of the disease until they are extremely ill since doing so would make them "easy prey" in the wild. To spot issues early and stop infections from spreading, we advise attentive monitoring of your pet rabbit, a healthy diet, current immunizations, and regular health checkups.

The following are the main prevalent issues/diseases we see in domestic rabbits:

- Expanded teeth
- Snuffles
- Hairballs
- Tumors in the uterine
- Myxomatosis
- Calicivirus (Rabbit Haemorrhagic Disease Virus)

Causes of overgrown teeth and symptoms

A rabbit's teeth continue to develop throughout its lifetime, and if it doesn't regularly grind them down by consuming fiber, we start to see sharp spikes emerging on its molar teeth, which may hurt its cheeks and tongue. As a result of the discomfort, many find it difficult or impossible to eat. In extreme instances, the incisors at the front of the mouth might curve around, making it impossible for rabbits to shut their mouths or even chew. A rabbit may pass away if they stop eating because its gut stops functioning.

Prevention

Your rabbit needs to consume 80–90% fiber in the form of oaten or grass hay. Leafy greens should make up the majority of the diet, with little to no pellets or other goodies.

Treatment

The only therapy for enlarged teeth is a general anesthetic along with flattening the teeth.

The cause of snuffles (pasteurellosis) and its symptoms

The Pasteurella multocida bacteria may be readily transmitted to your rabbit by close contact with an infected rabbit. The sickness is known as "snuffles" because the germs may affect the eyes (discharge, redness, squinting) and/or nose (sneezing, discharge). Infections caused by Pasteurella may also affect other parts of the body, such as the ears (which can cause a head tilt), abscesses (which appear as lumps on the body), and uterine infections.

Prevention

When the immune system is under stress—for example, when a new food or pet is introduced, or if there is overcrowding—certain strains of the bacteria may stay dormant in the rabbit's nasal passage. Reduced stress for infected rabbits and quarantining fresh rabbits are effective approaches to stop the spread of the illness or return of symptoms.

Treatment

An extensive and sometimes recurrent course of antibiotics is necessary for treatment. If an abscess develops, surgery may sometimes be necessary.

Trichobezoars (Hairballs): Cause and clinical symptoms

A rabbit's stomach often contains hair because they groom themselves. Hair must, however, be able to pass through the gut because rabbits cannot vomit. If it can't, it will create a blockage and cause significant problems. Because they are so frequent, hairballs should always be suspected in any rabbit that is sluggish and not eating.

Prevention

A high-fiber diet is a fantastic preventive technique since hairballs are more likely to develop into a problem if there is a problem with the gastrointestinal system (gut stasis) or if they are not getting enough fiber in their diet.

Treatment

In cases when the hairball blocks the intestines, surgery is sometimes the only option for therapy. Additionally helpful is medication that stimulates the stomach.

Causes of uterine tumors and clinical symptoms

Uterine adenocarcinoma, which may affect whole female rabbits, should be investigated if an undesexed female rabbit falls ill. Lethargy, aggressive behavior, mammary gland cysts, and blood-stained vaginal discharge are a few of the most prevalent clinical symptoms.

Prevention

Early desexing between 4-6 months.

Desexing is a kind of treatment, preferably before the cancer spreads throughout the body.

Causes and symptoms of myxomatosis

The virus that causes myxomatosis may be spread by fleas, mosquitoes, or by intimate contact between an infected and a susceptible rabbit. Swelling and drainage from the eyes, nose and anogenital area are symptoms of the condition.

Prevention

Unfortunately, Australia does not provide any vaccinations. Purchase a rabbit hutch that is mosquito-proof or bring your rabbit inside at dawn and dusk when there are more mosquitoes around. It might be helpful to use flea treatment, and when introducing fresh rabbits, keep them apart for at least two weeks.

Treatment
The condition always results in death.
Virus of Rabbit Haemorrhagic Disease (previously known as Rabbit Calicivirus)

Cause and medical symptoms
Mosquitoes, flies, and/or direct or indirect contact with an infected rabbit are the main vectors for the propagation of the Rabbit Haemorrhagic Disease Virus (formerly known as Rabbit Calicivirus).

RHDV virus presently comes in four strains (RHDV1, RHDVa, RHDV2, and RHDV1 K5). In the first week of March 2017, the RHDV 1 K5 virus will be made available throughout the country. The release of this virus is a biocontrol strategy being used to manage wild European rabbits.

Within 48–72 hours of infection, the illness in most adult rabbits advances quickly from fever and lethargy to abrupt death. For the RHDV, the incubation period lasts one to three days. Most rabbits won't have any RHDV outward symptoms.

The clinical symptoms include an inability to concentrate, restlessness, fatigue, and fever. The illness results in abrupt liver damage and irregular blood clotting as a consequence. Due to internal hemorrhages and/or the restriction of the blood flow to essential organs, this condition has the potential to be lethal. RHDV causes 70 to 90% of vulnerable rabbits to die.

By immunizing your rabbit, you may prevent:
Provide defense against RHDV1

The little study that has been done suggests that it does provide defense against RHDV1 K5.
Protection against RHDVa and RHDV2 may or may not be present, and not in every rabbit.

Adult rabbits get vaccinations every six months. Adult rabbits that are either past due for a vaccine or have never had one must get two shots, one month apart. Young rabbit kittens may start receiving vaccinations as early as four weeks old, then every month until they are 12 weeks old, and then every six months after that.

In addition to immunization, we advise:
keeping domestic and wild rabbits apart both directly and indirectly.
If there is a chance that wild rabbits would contaminate the grass, avoid cutting it and feeding it to rabbits.
Between handling rabbits, wash your hands with warm, soapy water.
Additionally crucial is effective insect management, which will lower the dangers of introducing both calicivirus and myxomatosis. Keeping rabbits inside and insect-proofing the hutch are two ways to manage insects. We also advise a monthly

application of a topical preventive for biting insects, but please see your veterinarian for advice on the proper dosing schedule.

It is important to separate infected rabbits while taking precautions to reduce environmental contamination.

Treatment

There is no available therapy.

Frequently, little changes in your rabbit's behavior might be a sign that a disease process is developing. It is advisable to get your rabbit examined by your veterinarian if you have observed any changes or are worried about anything they have been doing. Your rabbit has a higher chance of enjoying a healthy life if issues are found sooner.

Chapter 6

7 Ways to Earn Additional Income from Rabbits: How to Raise Rabbits for Profit

Raising rabbits for profit is a no-brainer if you are new to animal husbandry and want to start with something modest and simple.

On your farm, you may grow a variety of animals, including rabbits, which are adaptable, relatively cheap to keep, and, of course, breed fast.

Apart from their cutely twitching noses, rabbits may make money in a variety of ways.

Combining all of the above might result in a new business venture for you, even if one revenue source alone might not provide a profit worth bragging about.

1. Selling meat from rabbits

It is quite common to consume rabbit meat in many different cultures across the globe. It hasn't, however, attained the kind of popularity it deserves in the US.

Rabbits generate a very lean white flesh. It provides more protein and less calories and fat. The main drawback is that, if you have a cardiovascular illness, eating rabbit meat may not be a smart idea due to its increased cholesterol content.

Rabbit meat has a flavor that is quite similar to that of chicken, but a little bit stronger.

Therefore, if you want to eat healthier meat, you should think about a rabbit. In addition, you can substitute rabbit for chicken in almost any recipe.

Having said that, unless they are high-end locations, it might be difficult to locate rabbit meat in neighborhood restaurants and grocery shops.

If you have the time and space, raising rabbits for meat is a very straightforward enterprise to start. It may be quite profitable, particularly if you want to sell your product as being bred on grass rather than in hutches and want to rear your rabbits on grass.

Rabbits for Meat Processing:

You must process your rabbits in line with any county-specific rules once they are mature enough for processing, often at approximately 12 weeks.

In most meat processing circumstances, rabbits are regarded as "poultry," thus many of the same regulations that apply to chickens also apply to them. However, you may need to look around and ask a lot of questions to figure out what's acceptable and what would result in a punishment.

There are two methods to prepare your rabbits:

- You at your farm.
- In a USDA-inspected establishment

How many rabbits you want to process and where you plan to sell the rabbit meat will determine where you do it.

To Whom You Should Sell Your Rabbit Meat:

As soon as your meat has been prepared, you should get it to the customer. Here are some suggestions for places to sell your rabbit meat:

• Family and friends
• Local farmers' markets
• Expensive or regional eateries
• Food markets
• Internet (lots of extra red tape here since you may be selling across state lines)
• Dog owners who feed their canines raw dog food
Commercial dog food manufacturers

Potential Earnings:

It is clear that the price you might earn per pound reflects the fact that rabbit is regarded as a delicacy.

For your rabbit meat, you may ask for about $6 per pound. It makes no difference whether you offer it as dog food or for human consumption. Because there is a great demand for rabbits, you may inquire how much it is worth and probably receive it.

2. Market for Rabbit Pellets

Naturally, the hide is a byproduct, if you will, of processing a rabbit for a meal. You may create something lovely out of this rabbit part that many crafters would like to have in their workspace rather than throwing it away.

Clothes, toys, and other goods are often made from the pelts of rabbits. If you have creative talent, you may produce your own works of art and market them to customers.

Rabbit skin tanning may be a time-consuming procedure, but with caution and expertise, it can become simpler. You can either learn how to do this yourself or hire someone to do it for you. Just keep in mind that outsourcing will reduce your profit margin.

To Whom Should I Sell Rabbit Pelts?
• Business Industry
• Homesteaders

• Crafters

Potential Earnings:

I never said that you would be able to earn a fortune from your rabbit fur, and some people would rather throw away the byproduct than attempt to market and sell it.

The price of a rabbit pelt may range from $1.50 to $30. The value of your hide will vary depending on some variables, including:

- Type of Rabbit
- Age of the Rabbit
- Tanner's Talent
- Fur color
- Size of the Pelt

- Additional preparatory elements (dyed, patterned, etc.)

3. Using rabbit fur for fiber sales

For commercial enterprises and craftspeople looking to create a delicate, silky product, rabbit fur is a premium material.

Long-haired rabbits, like the Angora Rabbit, have their fur sheared, or hand-plucked, as opposed to the complete tanned skin.

If you want to raise rabbits for profit but don't want to kill them for food, you might start shearing your pet Angora rabbits and sell the fiber for a little profit.

For individuals interested in animal husbandry, keeping rabbits is often a simple endeavor; nevertheless, the Angora rabbit needs a little more care than a New Zealand rabbit (which is typically raised for meat). You must care for fiber almost every day if you want it to be lovely. If not properly cared for, long-haired rabbit breeds have a propensity to grow matted, which may be uncomfortable for the rabbit and raise the risk of illness and parasites.

Who to Sell Fiber from Rabbits To:
• Etsy
• Antique shops
• Crafters
• Spinners, knitters, and fiber artists
• Textile Mills
• Yarn stores

Potential Earnings:

Angora fiber may be sold for as little as $7 per ounce and as much as $16 or more. Once again, a few things will affect the prices you may charge and the willingness of customers to pay, factors like as

• Hand plucking—much preferable to shearing!

• A kind of rabbit

• The rabbit's age

• Fur color

4. Marketing Fertilizer Ready for Use Contains Rabbit Manure

Because it is high in nitrogen and can be applied directly to plants without causing the foliage to burn, rabbit dung is a fantastic fertilizer.

So, using nutrient-rich rabbit dung may be done immediately rather than needing to wait months to utilize fertilizer from other animals!

Buyers of Rabbit Manure:

• Gardeners

• Interested Farmers

• Landscape Contractors

Potential Earnings:

For a 40lb bag, I've seen rabbit dung prices range from $0 to $45. Now, if the manure has been aged or composted with worms, some individuals will pay extra (see below). Along with your location, supply and demand are other factors.

Therefore, although most just give it away for free out of a desire to get rid of it, others are earning a fortune off of their rabbits' waste (the $45 price tag is NOT the norm).

5. Construct a worm farm using rabbit waste

Worms may be added to the mix if you want to squeeze every last bit of utility out of your rabbitry enterprise.

Yes, you may employ worms and vermicomposting to assist compost waste, control smells, and perhaps generate additional cash.

Who Should I Sell Worms To?

You may utilize worms like nightcrawlers since you'll be utilizing them to:

- Fishermen
- Bait stores
- Those who make use of compost bins

Potential Earnings:
You probably never imagined that you might earn some extra money by gathering worms from your manure pile, but it is possible!

Earthworms, also known as nightcrawlers, can be sold for about $31 per pound. Though worms don't weigh much, so it can take some time to collect a pound of wrigglers. and plenty of feces.

If you fish, you are aware of how expensive worms are. A lot of bait stores charge $2 for a dozen, and you may as well.

6. Pet Rabbit Sales

You may always sell your bunnies as pets or breeders to those who are simply looking for a cuddly bunny to cuddle.

If your neighborhood pet businesses are seeking a reliable source of rabbits, you may inquire with them. Just keep in mind that pet shops need to make a profit on your buns and won't demand to pay more than $15 per bunny.

Additionally, pet shops often don't care if your rabbit is purebred or mixed-breed, so it won't matter if your Flemish Giant won first place at the regional fair and her offspring are valued at $80. They'll ask for $10 from you.

However, depending on the use and quality of your stock, you may sell your live bunnies for anywhere between $20 and $100 if you strategically arrange your promotion (ahem, Easter and fair season).

Because they want to learn about animal husbandry and purchase the winning rabbit, 4-H members are excellent customers. And I swear to you, witnessing a youngster choose their new pet is utterly priceless, regardless of how much money you earn with your bunnies.

7. **Pinkie selling**

Selling baby kits to snake owners and pet shops may make you cringe a bit, but if you want to add another source of money to your list, you may do so.

If you don't want to, you may sell the ones who perished from your most recent kindling instead of bringing live ones to the pet shop (litter of rabbits).

Large rabbitries often include stillborns and does who neglect their young. Large litters often have problems because the does do not have enough milk to feed their whole family.
If a kit is found to be dead but has not been for a long time, you may freeze it and sell it when you have enough.

No one wants a rotting pinkie, so be careful to check often.

Who Should Buy Pinkies?

- Snake Keepers
- Pet stores

Potential Earnings:

Per pinkie, around $3.

You should now be aware that there are several possibilities available for growing rabbits for profit. Additionally, you may combine a few to create several sources of revenue. Who could refuse that?